Getting Started with D3

Mike Dewar

O'REILLY®

Beijing · Cambridge · Farnham · Köln · Sebastopol · Tokyo

Getting Started with D3
by Mike Dewar

Published by O'Reilly Media, Inc., 1005 Gravenstein Highway North, Sebastopol, CA 95472.

O'Reilly books may be purchased for educational, business, or sales promotional use. Online editions are also available for most titles (*http://my.safaribooksonline.com*). For more information, contact our corporate/institutional sales department: 800-998-9938 or *corporate@oreilly.com*.

Editors: Julie Steele and Meghan Blanchette	**Cover Designer:** Karen Montgomery
Production Editor: Melanie Yarbrough	**Interior Designer:** David Futato
	Illustrator: Robert Romano

Revision History for the First Edition:
   2012-06-26   First release
See *http://oreilly.com/catalog/errata.csp?isbn=9781449328795* for release details.

ISBN: 978-1-449-32879-5

[LSI]

1340633573

Table of Contents

Preface

The D3 JavaScript library allows us to make beautiful, interactive, browser-based data visualizations. By exposing the underlying elements of a web page in the context of a data set, D3 gives you complete control over your visualization. This fantastic power, though, comes with a short, sharp learning curve—a curve that this book aims to overcome.

By working through a collection of data sets, we will build up a series of visualizations, exposing new D3 concepts along the way. The data for this book has been gathered and made publicly available by the New York Metropolitan Transit Authority (MTA) and details various aspects of New York's transit system, comprising of historical tables, live data streams, and geographical information. By the end of the book, we will have visited some of the core aspects of D3, and will be properly equipped to build basic, interactive data visualizations on the Web.

Who This Book Is For

This is a little book aimed at the data scientist: someone who has data to visualize and who wants to use the power of the modern web browser to give his visualizations additional impact. This might be an academic who wants to escape the confines of the printed article, a statistician who needs to share their impressive results with the rest of her company, or the designer who wants to get his info-viz out far and wide on the Internet.

It's assumed, therefore, that the reader is happy with coding and manipulating data. We will not cover any statistics or modelling, we will not stray outside the JavaScript or SVG we need for the visualizations, and we won't discuss aesthetics past what we consider basic good taste. These are important topics and we point to *Machine Learning for Hackers* by Drew Conway and John Myles White, *JavaScript: The Good Parts* by Douglas Crockford, *SVG Essentials* by J. David Eisenberg, and *Visualizing Data* by Ben Fry for these important introductions.

Conventions Used in This Book

The following typographical conventions are used in this book:

Italic

    Indicates new terms, URLs, email addresses, filenames, and file extensions.

`Constant width`

    Used for program listings, as well as within paragraphs to refer to program elements such as variable or function names, databases, data types, environment variables, statements, and keywords.

`Constant width bold`

    Shows commands or other text that should be typed literally by the user.

`Constant width italic`

    Shows text that should be replaced with user-supplied values or by values determined by context.

    This icon signifies a tip, suggestion, or general note.

    This icon indicates a warning or caution.

Using Code Examples

This book is here to help you get your job done. In general, you may use the code in this book in your programs and documentation. You do not need to contact us for permission unless you're reproducing a significant portion of the code. For example, writing a program that uses several chunks of code from this book does not require permission. Selling or distributing a CD-ROM of examples from O'Reilly books does require permission. Answering a question by citing this book and quoting example code does not require permission. Incorporating a significant amount of example code from this book into your product's documentation does require permission.

We appreciate, but do not require, attribution. An attribution usually includes the title, author, publisher, and ISBN. For example: "*Getting Started with D3* by Mike Dewar (O'Reilly). Copyright 2012 Mike Dewar, 978-1-449-32879-5."

If you feel your use of code examples falls outside fair use or the permission given above, feel free to contact us at *permissions@oreilly.com*.

Safari® Books Online

Safari Books Online (*www.safaribooksonline.com*) is an on-demand digital library that delivers expert content in both book and video form from the world's leading authors in technology and business.

Technology professionals, software developers, web designers, and business and creative professionals use Safari Books Online as their primary resource for research, problem solving, learning, and certification training.

Safari Books Online offers a range of product mixes and pricing programs for organizations, government agencies, and individuals. Subscribers have access to thousands of books, training videos, and prepublication manuscripts in one fully searchable database from publishers like O'Reilly Media, Prentice Hall Professional, Addison-Wesley Professional, Microsoft Press, Sams, Que, Peachpit Press, Focal Press, Cisco Press, John Wiley & Sons, Syngress, Morgan Kaufmann, IBM Redbooks, Packt, Adobe Press, FT Press, Apress, Manning, New Riders, McGraw-Hill, Jones & Bartlett, Course Technology, and dozens more. For more information about Safari Books Online, please visit us online.

How to Contact Us

Please address comments and questions concerning this book to the publisher:

> O'Reilly Media, Inc.
> 1005 Gravenstein Highway North
> Sebastopol, CA 95472
> 800-998-9938 (in the United States or Canada)
> 707-829-0515 (international or local)
> 707-829-0104 (fax)

We have a web page for this book, where we list errata, examples, and any additional information. You can access this page at:

> *http://oreil.ly/get_started_D3*

To comment or ask technical questions about this book, send email to:

> *bookquestions@oreilly.com*

For more information about our books, courses, conferences, and news, see our website at *http://www.oreilly.com*.

Find us on Facebook: *http://facebook.com/oreilly*

Follow us on Twitter: *http://twitter.com/oreillymedia*

Watch us on YouTube: *http://www.youtube.com/oreillymedia*

Acknowledgements

I'd like to thank Mike Bostock for putting together such a fine library, and for his help and comments. My good friends and colleagues Brian Eoff, John Myles White, Drew Conway, Max Shron, and Gabriel Gaster have all helped tremendously with technical comments (and the occasional British to American English conversion). My editor and conscience Meghan Blanchette has been remarkably effective, somehow coaxing this little book out of me without yelling. Most of all, I'd like to thank my fiancee Monica Vakil for her love, patience, and support.

CHAPTER 1

Introduction

Visualizing data is now an old trade. We have, in one way or another, been visualizing collected data for a long time—the year of this writing is the 143rd birthday of Minard's famous Napoleon's March flow map shown in Figure 1-1. Lately, though, we've gone into overdrive, as the amount of data we capture increases without bound and our ability to glean insights from it develops and matures. The Internet, combined with the latest generation of browsers, gives us a fantastic opportunity to take our urge to visualize to the next level: to create live, interactive graphics that have the opportunity to reach millions of people.

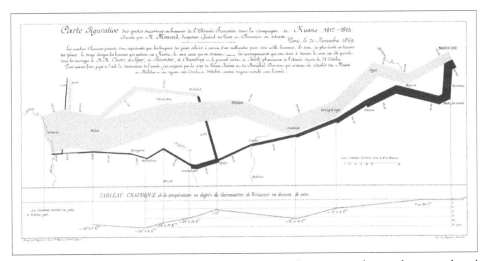

Figure 1-1. Minard's flow map depicting Napoleon's dwindling army as he marches toward, and retreats from, Moscow. "Drawn up by M. Minard, Inspector General of Bridges and Roads in retirement. Paris, November 20, 1869."

JavaScript is the language of the modern browser. As such, it is the most installed language in the world: the one language you can be confident is installed on the user's computer. Similarly, all modern browsers (with the introduction of IE9 in 2011) can render Scalable Vector Graphics (SVG), including mobile devices that are unable to render Flash. Together, the combination of JavaScript and SVG allows us to create sophisticated charts that are accessible by a majority of Internet users. And, thanks to D3, bringing these technologies together is a straightforward task.

D3

D3 is a JavaScript library written by Mike Bostock, created as a successor to an earlier visualization toolkit called Protovis. The D3 library allows us to manipulate elements of a web page in the context of a data set. These elements can be HTML, SVG, or Canvas elements, and can be introduced, removed, or edited according to the contents of the data set. So, for example, to create a scatter graph, we use D3 to arrange SVG `circle` elements such that their `cx` and `cy` attributes are set to the x- and y-values of the elements in a data set, scaled to map from their natural units into pixels.

A huge benefit of how D3 exposes the designer directly to the web page is that the existing technology in the browser can be leveraged without having to create a whole new plotting language. This appears both when selecting elements, which is performed using CSS selectors (users of JQuery will find many of the idioms underlying D3 very familiar), and when styling elements, which is performed using normal CSS. This allows the designer to use the existing tools that have been developed for web design—most notably Firefox's Firebug and Chrome's Developer Tools.

Instead of creating a traditional visualization toolkit, which typically places a heavy wrapper between the designer and the web page, D3 is focused on providing helper functions to deal with mundane tasks, such as creating axes and axis ticks, or advanced tasks such as laying out graph visualizations or chord diagrams. This means that, once over D3's initial learning curve, the designer is opened up to a very rich world of modern, interactive and animated data visualization.

The Basic Setup

The D3 library can be downloaded from *http://d3js.org*. It will be assumed that the *d3.js* file lives in the folder that contains the HTML for each example.

All the examples in this book rely on a common HTML and JavaScript structure, which is shown in Example 1-1.

Example 1-1. Basic page setup used throughout this book

```
<!DOCTYPE html>
<html>
<head>
    <meta charset="utf-8">
    <script src="d3.js"></script> ❶
    <script>
    function draw(data) { ❷
```

```
        "use strict"; ❸
        // badass visualization code goes here
    }
    </script>
</head>
<body>
    <script>
        d3.json("data/some_data.json", draw); ❹
    </script>
</body>
</html>
```

❶ The D3 library is always included to give our visualizations access to the D3 methods.

❷ The rest of the book will focus on this function, which we will always call draw. This is a function with one argument; it is called once the data has been downloaded to the client. It will contain the bulk of the code necessary to create the visualization.

❸ All the JavaScript will satisfy the JSLint tool, available at *http://www.jslint.com/*. D3 encourages the use of the "cascade" JavaScript coding style, making it easy to write well-formed JavaScript. The "use strict"; line instructs the browser to apply a strict interpretation of the JavaScript rules which, by making us write cleaner code, allows us to avoid confusing bugs.

❹ The d3.json() function makes an HTTP GET request to a JSON file at the URL described by its first argument and once the data has been downloaded, will then call the function passed as the second argument. This second argument is a callback function (which we will always call draw), which is passed, as its only parameter, the contents of the JSON having been turned into an object or an array, whichever is appropriate. Although D3 can read both XML and CSV, we remain constant throughout the book and stick to JSON.

The approach taken in this book is to expose the reader to the process of building up the visualizations. This means that the first few steps of the process can result in some ugly, incomprehensible pages, which are subsequently styled into shape. As such, all the CSS is detailed in the examples and tends to be explained after the elements of the visualization have been specified.

The New York Metropolitan Transit Authority Data Set

New York is an incredibly large, incredibly dense city with a lot of people constantly moving around. As such, it has evolved an intricate transport network, large parts of which are managed by the Metropolitan Transit Authority (MTA). The MTA is responsible for the local trains, subways, buses, bridges, and tunnels that move over 11 million people a day through the five boroughs and beyond.

The MTA has made a large amount of data associated with the running of this network publicly available. This has, in turn, generated a vibrant developer community that is able to build on top of this data that enable the residents of NYC to interact more efficiently with the transport network their tax dollars support.

We will use this data as inspiration for each example in this book. Each of the examples herein use one or more data files released by the MTA, which can be found at *http://www.mta.info/developers/*. This is a great resource that, as well as providing up-to-date data sets, also points to the invaluable user group that has formed around this data.

Cleaning the Data

The source code associated with this book lives in two directories, links to which can be found on the book's catalog page (*http://oreil.ly/get_started_D3*). The /code directory holds Python code that converts the MTA data, which is in many different formats, to well-formed JSON. Processing the data is not the focus of this book, and the examples can be followed without needing to run or understand the Python code. This code also has the potential to go out of date as the MTA updates its data files.

> D3 is not a great tool for cleaning data. In general, while it is certainly possible to use JavaScript to clean up data, it is not wise to perform this on the client machine in the browser. For this book Python has been used to clean up the data prior to developing the visualizations as it has many mature tools for parsing XML, CSV, and JSON, and is an all around good tool for this sort of thing.

The /viz folder holds the HTML files for each visualization. We shall focus on this section of the code for the rest of the book. The cleaned up JSON data is stored in /viz/data. Some of these files are quite large, so be warned before loading them up in a text editor!

> Time spent forming clean, well-structured JSON can save you a lot of heartache down the road. Make sure any JSON you use satisfies *http://jsonlint.com* at the very least. Performing cleaning or data analysis in the browser is not only a frustrating programming task, but can also make your visualization less responsive.

Micha's Golden Rule

Micha Gorelick, a data scientist in NYC, coined the following rule:

> Do not store data in the keys of a JSON blob.

This is Micha's Golden Rule; it should always be followed when forming JSON for use in D3, and will save you many confusing hours. This means that one should never form JSON like the following:

```
{
    "bob": 20,
    "alice": 23,
    "drew": 30
}
```

Here we are storing data in both the key (name) and the value (age). This is perfectly valid JSON, but breaks Micha's Golden Rule, which is bad. Instead, we would form the following as a list:

```
[
    {
        "name": "bob",
        "age": 20
    },
    {
        "name": "alice",
        "age": 23
    },
    {
        "name": "drew",
        "age": 30
    }
]
```

Here, we store data only in the values, and the keys indicate only what the data represents. If you are in the unfortunate position of having JSON that breaks Micha's Golden Rule, consider using d3.entries() to make the conversion.

Serving the Data

As noted above, d3.json() makes HTTP GET requests to a web server. We therefore need a web server running to handle these requests and serve up our JSON. A simple way of solving this is to use Python's SimpleHTTPServer to serve up all the HTML and JSON files to the browser. On Linux and OS X, you almost definitely have Python installed. On Windows, you can download Python from *http://python.org*.

To start up the server, use a terminal (Linux or OS X) or command prompt (Windows) to navigate to the viz folder and type the following:

```
python -m SimpleHTTPServer 8000
```

This starts up an HTTP server on port 8000. If you open up a browser and point it at *http://localhost:8000*, you will see all the example HTML files for this book, as well as the data directory that contains all the cleaned up JSON files.

 There are any number of ways of serving HTTP files; using Python is a pretty simple cross-platform approach.

Having started an HTTP server, all the requests for data we make will be to this server, which will happily serve up the data. By keeping our paths relative to the viz folder we will be able to transplant any code we write to a more serious production server to share what we write with the world.

CHAPTER 2

The Enter Selection

Selections are a core concept in D3. Based on CSS selectors, they allow us to select elements of the web page and modify, append to, or remove these items in concert with a data set. In this chapter, we will use selections of HTML elements to create two very simple visualizations: a list and a basic bar chart.

Both visualizations share a common structure: we select the body of the page, we append a container element and then, for each element of the data set, we append a visual element whose properties are defined by the data. This is the basic pattern by which we build up more complex visualizations. Mastering this pattern forms the bulk of D3's learning curve.

Building a Simple Subway Train Status Board

Knowing when the trains are running in New York can make all the difference to your day. Subway trains are subject to construction work, scheduling changes, and unforeseen delays. And at over five million rides on a weekday, delays can affect a huge group of people.

Happily, the New York MTA makes live information available, updated every minute, indicating the status of each subway line. This release of public data has generated a wonderful ecosystem of applications developed for smartphones and the Web. Our first example adds a (modest) contribution to this ecosystem, using D3 to make a list showing the status of each train. Here is the process we've followed:

1. Download the data, which is in XML format, from *http://www.mta.info/status/serv iceStatus.txt*.
2. Extract the subset of the XML that we are interested in, and convert the XML to JSON to give us **/data/service_status.json**.
3. Modify our template (Example 1-1) to request the service status data:

   ```
   d3.json("data/service_status.json", draw)
   ```
4. Write the **draw** function.

5. Serve the files using `python -m SimpleHTTPServer 8000`.

6. Point a browser at *http://localhost:8000* and enjoy!

The service status data downloaded from the MTA comes nice and clean, so all we really need for this first example is to convert the XML to JSON and subset it. Having converted the file to JSON the non-subway aspects of the file are discarded and the resulting file can be found in the data directory as `service_status.json`. The status for a single line looks like the following:

```
{
    "status": ["GOOD SERVICE"],
    "name": ["123"],
    "url": [null],
    "text": ["..."],
    "plannedworkheadline": [null],
    "Time": [" 7:35AM"],
    "Date": ["12/15/2011"]
}
```

The draw Function

Our first `draw` function has a simple goal: create a list of all the subway lines in New York along with their service status. From D3's point of view, this translates into creating an `<li>` element for every element in the data set, whose text content is the name of the line and the service status.

The code for the draw function is shown immediately below. Remember that this function sits inside the template in Example 1-1. Roughly, we select the body element, append a `<ul>` element to store our list, and then, for each element in the data, we append an `<li>` element with the required text. How D3 accomplishes this can seem a bit odd, so we shall step through each of these lines carefully:

```
function draw(data) {
    "use strict";
    d3.select("body")
      .append("ul")
      .selectAll("li")
      .data(data)
      .enter()
      .append("li")
        .text(function (d) {
            return d.name + ": " + d.status;
        });
}
```

This style of programming is called "method chaining" or a "cascade": each method returns a selection which in turn has methods that return a selection. Practically, a selection is an array of elements blessed with special methods that allow us to perform operations on all elements in the selection.

The cascade begins using d3.select("body"), which selects the body element of the page, ready for us to append new elements to. We then append an unnumbered list to the body, which creates a <ul> element in the page. Like the select method, the append method returns a selection except this time it's the unnumbered list that's been selected.

We then do a slightly odd thing: we selectAll list elements on the page, even though we know there aren't any. This prepares the way for new list elements to enter the visualization. Practically, this creates the *empty selection*, which is an array with no elements, but that has been blessed with a data method, allowing it to accept data.

The data method joins the empty selection with each element of the data set. This results in a selection that is an array with as many elements as we have data points (subway lines). We're still not quite there: this array's elements are all empty, however this selection has a new enter method.

The enter method returns a selection whose array contains the data for all the new elements we're going to create; all the elements for which we have data but don't already have items on the page. This is called the *enter selection*.

 At first glance, the .enter() method can seem a little superfluous. Why doesn't the .data() method simply return the array with the data already in it? The reason that these are two separate methods is that .data() initializes a selection, like setting a stage, and then .enter() selects only those elements that have a data point but that don't already exist on the screen—those elements that are going to enter the stage. This is very important for dynamic pages, where elements come and go. In this book's examples, we only ever use the .enter() method in its simplest incarnation, as in the preceding example. For more details on this aspect of D3, check out *http://bost.ocks.org/mike/join/*.

In this first example, we don't have any elements on the page at all, so the .enter() method returns a selection containing data for all 11 data elements. This enter selection is now ready for us to append elements to it.

Developer Tools

Google Chrome's Developer Tools or Firefox's Firebug are an essential part of a web developer's toolset. If you are investigating JavaScript for the first time, especially in the context of drawing visualizations, your first experience of the developer tools is like a breath of fresh air.

In Chrome, to access the developer tools, navigate to View→Developer→Developer Tools. In Firefox, you can download Firebug from *http://getfirebug.com/*. Once it's installed, it will be available in the View menu.

In order to get your head around the d3.select(), it's really useful to run these commands in the developer tool's console so you can get a firsthand view of what's actually going on. While you have the visualization open in a browser, try opening the console and stepping through the preceding commands. To be able to access the data in the console, use `d3.json("data/some_data.json", function(data){d=data})` to assign the data to a global variable called d. Then try, for example:

```
d3.select("body")
    .selectAll("p")
    .data(d)
```

and have a look at the output. You can build up the enter selection command by command, interrogating the selection object as you go.

Finally, we need to tell D3 what to do with each element of the entering selection we've just created. For this visualization, we append an `<li>` element to the enter selection whose text contains the name of the line and its status.

To access individual elements of the data, we need to write a callback function as the `text`'s second argument. This function is passed the current element in the data set and the index of that element. For this example, our callback accesses two elements of the data—the `name` and `status`—and simply concatenates them, returning the result. This results in the nice and simple list in Figure 2-1.

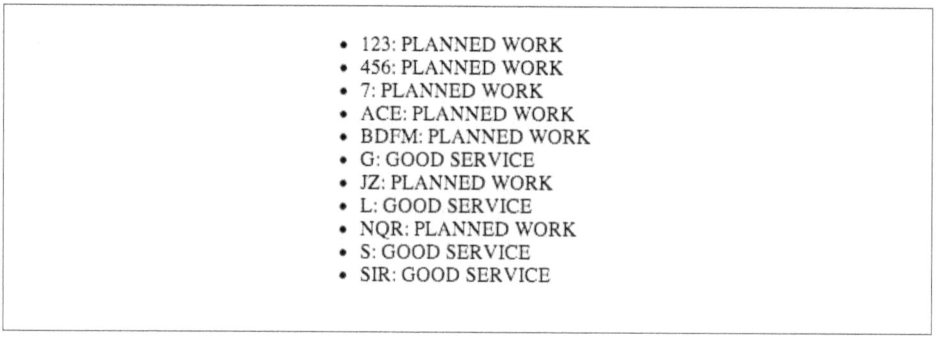

- 123: PLANNED WORK
- 456: PLANNED WORK
- 7: PLANNED WORK
- ACE: PLANNED WORK
- BDFM: PLANNED WORK
- G: GOOD SERVICE
- JZ: PLANNED WORK
- L: GOOD SERVICE
- NQR: PLANNED WORK
- S: GOOD SERVICE
- SIR: GOOD SERVICE

Figure 2-1. Status list

Adding Data-Dependent Style

Our list, while functional, is a little boring. We can spruce it up a little without much effort, and make it easier to grok. Let's set the font weight of the lines with "GOOD SERVICE" to normal, and those without to bold:

```
d3.selectAll("li")
    .style("font-weight", function (d) {
        if (d.status == "GOOD SERVICE"){
            return "normal";
        } else {
            return "bold";
        }
    })
```

This code lives inside the `draw` function, below the code that draws the list. It selects the `<li>` elements we've already created and adjusts the style accordingly.

Notice that the data is "sticky"—the individual data points are associated with those elements on the page that they were bound to in the entering selection. This means we can select all the list elements and modify their style according to the data. Our new, slightly sexier list now has data-dependent style, as shown in Figure 2-2.

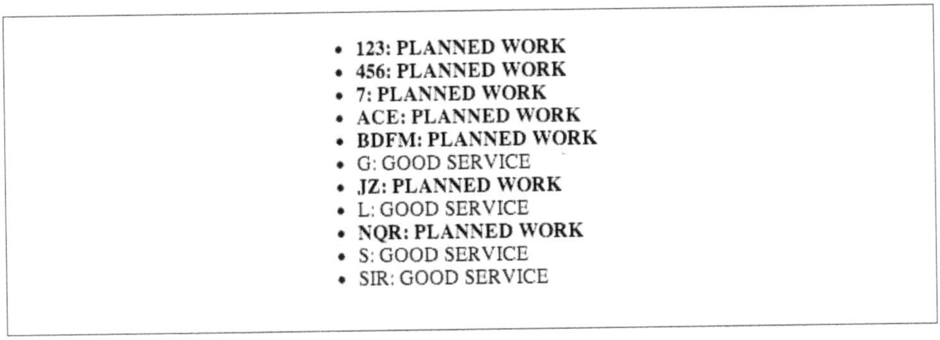

- **123: PLANNED WORK**
- **456: PLANNED WORK**
- **7: PLANNED WORK**
- **ACE: PLANNED WORK**
- **BDFM: PLANNED WORK**
- G: GOOD SERVICE
- **JZ: PLANNED WORK**
- L: GOOD SERVICE
- **NQR: PLANNED WORK**
- S: GOOD SERVICE
- SIR: GOOD SERVICE

Figure 2-2. Status list with data-dependent font weight

Graphing Mean Daily Plaza Traffic

Every morning many tens of thousands of commuters drive their cars over bridges and through tunnels into Manhattan, passing through one of 11 areas where a toll is collected, known as plazas. Every day, the MTA counts how many cars paid cash and how many paid electronically and makes this data available to the public. Our next example will be to make a bar chart that shows the daily mean traffic through each plaza.

The data is available from the MTA site as `TBTA_DAILY_PLAZA_TRAFFIC.csv`, which is a relatively well-behaved CSV file. All we had to do was turn the counts into integers, find the daily mean, and introduce the name for each plaza. While the plaza names weren't available straight away, the wonderful "MTA developer resources" user group made these available upon request. The resulting JSON is called `plaza_traffic.json`, and a single element in that array looks like the following:

```
{
    "count": 26774.09756097561,
    "id": 1,
    "name": "Robert F. Kennedy Bridge Bronx Plaza"
},
```

Using div Tags to Create a Horizontal Bar Chart

For this example, we will apply the same pattern for laying out our chart elements as the preceding list. Instead of using list items to build up our visualization, here we are using div tags with specified widths to draw the rectangles that make up the bar chart. Other than this, the structure of the code is nearly identical!

```
function draw(data) {
  d3.select("body")
    .append("div")
      .attr("class","chart")
    .selectAll(".bar")
    .data(data.cash)
    .enter()
    .append("div")
      .attr("class","bar")
      .style("width", function(d){return d.count/100 + "px"})
      .style("outline", "1px solid black")
      .text(function(d){return Math.round(d.count)});
}
```

Here the containing element is a div tag, whose class is set to "chart." This allows us to select it later, and apply any styles that are appropriate for the whole chart. We then selectAll the div tags whose class is bar—as before this is an empty selection. We join the empty selection to our data and then generate the entering selection—an array with one element per data point.

To the entering selection we append div tags with class bar whose width and text elements are specified according to the count property in our data. As this count is on the order of tens of thousands, it is divided by 100 to convert the vehicle count to a manageable number of pixels (note that scales will be dealt with in a saner manner in the next chapter).

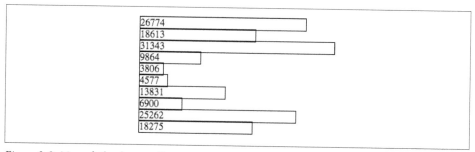

Figure 2-3. Mean daily plaza traffic

This results in the bar chart shown in Figure 2-3. By simply arranging div tags, we already have a pretty serviceable bar chart. However, it is fantastically ugly, and unlikely to make its readers all that happy.

Styling the Visualization using CSS

We shall remove the outline style from our JavaScript, and place the following CSS in the style tag at the top of the HTML:

```
div.chart{
    font-family:sans-serif;
    font-size:0.7em;
}
div.bar {
    background-color:DarkRed;
    color:white;
    height:3em;
    line-height:3em;
    padding-right:1em;
    margin-bottom:2px;
    text-align:right;
}
```

which styles the chart in a much more pleasing manner, as shown in Figure 2-4. It's important to realize how much of the design of the visualization is simply styling; by exposing the underlying elements of the web page, D3 gives us very tight control over the styling of the page, using the already well-developed language of CSS. This also opens up the potential for styling the visualization differently for different platforms or different users, simply by swapping out the CSS.

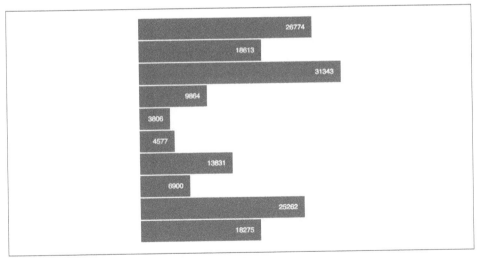

Figure 2-4. Mean daily plaza traffic—with a bit of CSS

Introducing Labels

As it stands, we can't learn much from this graph. All we really know is that some plazas have a lot more traffic than others; it is crying out for some labels. To introduce the labels we stored in the JSON, we are going to have to break up the flow of our code a little.

 In this example, we use floating `div` tags to build up our visualization. This is appealing as we don't have to grapple with anything other than HTML, and we can feel confident that this graph will display nicely on older browsers. It does mean that we have to be careful with the browser layout rules, and means our JavaScript is a little more complex than necessary. It also means we are using CSS to control the size of our bars, which is problematic as user stylesheets could change the shape of our visualizations! SVG-based visualizations, which we use in the following chapters, don't suffer these problems.

We would like to place the name of the plaza next to each bar. As the name is neatly stored in the JSON, we can simply make another `div` tag whose `text` attribute is set to the name of the plaza. But to get this on the lefthand side of the bar means we will have to draw it first, before the `div` tag that makes up bar. And, as both the label and the bar share a common data element, it is useful to create one container `div` element per data element to which we can append labels, then bars.

So we need to start over, first by building up a set of `div` tags, one per data point:

```
d3.select("body")
  .append("div")
    .attr("class", "chart")
  .selectAll("div.line")
  .data(data.cash)
  .enter()
  .append("div")
    .attr("class","line");
```

Hopefully this is starting to look a little familiar: we select the body of the page, append our chart `div`, select all the `div` tags with class `line` (of which none exist), join the empty selection with data, enter the selection, and append a `div` tag of class `line` for each element of the data. Our HTML now looks like the following:

```
<div class="chart">
    <div class="line"/>
    <div class="line"/>
    <div class="line"/>
    ...
    <div class="line"/>
</div>
```

With this structure in place it's simple to go ahead and append a label to each line:

```
d3.selectAll("div.line")
  .append("div")
    .attr("class","label")
    .text(function(d){return d.name});
```

and then append a bar to each line:

```
d3.selectAll("div.line")
  .append("div")
    .attr("class","bar")
    .style("width", function(d){return d.count/100 + "px"})
    .text(function(d){return Math.round(d.count)});
```

As mentioned in the previous example, the data associated with the selection d3.selec
tAll("div.line") is "sticky," so we can refer to it each time we make that selection.
The data is passed down to all the children of the selection, which means that the
div.label and div.bar can access the same data as div.line.

Finally, to stop the bars and labels flowing crazily around each other we need to impose
a bit more style. We give the div.bar a nice big left margin, and then the label looks
like the following:

```
div.label {
    height:3em;
    line-height:3em;
    padding-right:1em;
    margin-bottom:2px;
    float:left;
    width:20em;
    text-align:right;
}
```

The float:left means that the bar will sit happily on the righthand side of the label;
fixing the width of the label means that all the bars will line up with each other nicely.
This all results in a richer visualization shown in Figure 2-5.

 If you download the data from the MTA yourself (which you should
most definitely do), don't be surprised if the data looks a lot different
to Figure 2-5! This is dynamic data—the mean traffic will undoubtedly
flow in interesting ways.

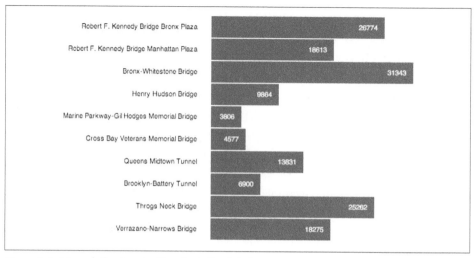

Figure 2-5. Mean daily plaza traffic—including labels

CHAPTER 3

Scales, Axes, and Lines

One of the basic problems we need to overcome when plotting on a web page is how to convert the values in our data into an appropriate representation in terms of pixels or colors. For statistical visualizations this can be a complicated process: we need to be able to deal with numerical and ordinal scales, log scales, time scales, and so on. The authors of D3 have made all this very easy, as we shall see in this chapter.

Bus Breakdown, Accident, and Injury

New York City has an intricate bus system that serves an incredible number of people every day. MTA's buses have to navigate a very busy city and so, inevitably, accidents will occur. The MTA makes its breakdown and accident data available to the public, so we are going to see if breakdowns, collisions, and customer accidents are related.

In order to do this, we will plot a basic scatter graph, which involves placing circles at specified locations on the web page. In the previous chapter, we used HTML elements (div tags) to build the bar chart; here we will instead use SVG elements to build a scatter chart.

Using SVG limits us to modern browsers. All versions of Internet Explorer up to and including version 8 failed to provide SVG support, though plug-ins that introduce support are available. Internet Explorer version 9 (released in March 2011) does include support, and most other popular browsers have had SVG support for half a decade or more at the time of this writing. Nonetheless, it is important to realize that SVG-based visualizations won't be viewable by all browsers.

The data is available at *http://www.mta.info/developers/data/Performance_XML_Data .zip* and has been processed to extract the "Collisions with Injury Rate," "Mean Distance Between Failures," and "Customer Accident Injury Rate." The file can be found in *data/bus_perf.json*, and an individual line in the data set looks like the following:

```
{
    "collision_with_injury": 3.2,
    "dist_between_fail": 3924.0,
    "customer_accident_rate": 2.12
}
```

A Tiny SVG Primer

SVG is an XML-based specification for drawing things. We've no space to go into SVG in detail here, but you absolutely need to know the following facts in order to proceed:

- All SVG elements should live inside an `svg` tag that takes as attributes `width` and `height`. Your visualization has to live inside this viewport—anything outside these bounds will exist in the DOM, but you won't be able to see them.

- The coordinates that SVG uses start at (0,0) in the top-left corner of the *enclosing element*. This can cause headaches for those of us used to plotting things from (0,0) in the bottom-left corner.

- Unlike the HTML elements, we specify all the aspects of SVG elements—like shape and location—as attributes in the tags, as opposed to using CSS. Each shape has a set of attributes that must be specified before the browser can render them.

- Having said this, it's important to realize that SVG, like other elements in the web page, can be styled using CSS! While CSS does not control the geometrical properties of the shapes, it can be used to control colors, strokes, fonts, and so on. This allows us to focus first on the layout and technical accuracy of a visualization, and leave the style until afterwards (or to our less aesthetically challenged friends and colleagues).

- In SVG, g stands for "group." We use g elements to group together other elements. We use this a lot to move groups of objects around. For example, we will create a "chart" group to bring together all the chart elements, which we could, were we so inclined, move around as one.

Using extent and scale to Map Data to Pixels

We're going to plot the collisions with injury rate against mean distances between failures as a scatter graph. We're going to use SVG `circle` elements to draw the points of the scatter graph, but apart from having to know a tiny bit about SVG the structure of the program is going to be the same as both the previous examples. What we need to overcome in this example is how to map the rate—which is typically less than 10— and the distance between failures— which is between 3000 and 5000—onto a position specified in pixels on the screen.

First, we set up the viewport dimensions. Our basic SVG viewport will be 700 pixels wide and 300 pixels tall. We set up a margin of 50 pixels, which will be enough space to contain axis ticks and tick labels:

```
var margin = 50,
    width = 700,
    height = 300;
```

 Setting up the SVG viewport in this way can lead to some little annoy-ances when setting up scales. In the following chapter, we will build up a more robust way of dealing with dimensions and margins.

We then follow the same pattern as shown in Chapter 2, except this time we contain all the visualization elements inside an SVG element. We set the `width` and `height` attributes of the SVG element before forming the enter selection and adding a circle for each data point:

```
d3.select("body")
  .append("svg")
    .attr("width", width)
    .attr("height", height)
  .selectAll("circle")
  .data(data)
  .enter()
  .append("circle");
```

To persuade the browser to render the circles, we need to specify the x- and y-location (relative to the top-left corner of the enclosing element, don't forget) of the circles and the radius of each one. This involves scaling our data such that it makes sense in terms of pixels. In the language of D3 this means we need to construct a function that maps from the data *domain* (input) onto a *range* (output) of pixels. This is exactly what the *scale* objects do.

First, we find the maximum and minimum values of the data, using `d3.extent`:

```
var x_extent = d3.extent(data, function(d){return d.collision_with_injury});
```

The function `d3.extent` is a convenience function that D3 provides that returns the minimum and the maximum values of its arguments, which in this case is the collisions with injury rate. We also specify, as the second argument to extent, an accessor function that chooses which attribute of the data to use when calculating the minimum and maximum values. We can then build the scale:

```
var x_scale = d3.scale.linear()
    .range([margin,width-margin])
    .domain(x_extent);
```

The `x_scale` now maps the extent of the data onto the range [40, 660]. This means that we can now use `x_scale` as a function that accepts numbers between the minimum and maximum values of the data and outputs numbers between 40 and 660.

We do the same thing for the y-axis, except that we take as the domain the extent of the distance between failure. The range is now from the height of the viewport down to the margin:

```
var y_extent = d3.extent(data, function(d){return d.dist_between_fail});

var y_scale = d3.scale.linear()
    .range([height-margin, margin])
    .domain(y_extent);
```

 Note that the domain for the y-scale is from the minimum to the maximum value in the data set, yet the range is from the maximum y-value in the viewport (300) to the margin value (50). This means we map the largest data point to 50 and the smallest data point to 300. While seeming odd at first, this is a result of the fact that viewport's origin is the top-left of the enclosing element, whereas we want our origin to be at the bottom-left! This is accomplished by our reverse mapping.

These two scales allow us to easily lay out the circles in the viewport, knowing that they will be sensibly positioned in the viewport within our margins. To use the scales, we treat them as functions that takes a data element as input and returns the correct position in pixels:

```
d3.selectAll("circle")
    .attr("cx", function(d){return x_scale(d.collision_with_injury)})
    .attr("cy", function(d){return y_scale(d.dist_between_fail)});
```

We must also specify the radius of the circles in order for the browser to render them. For now, we shall just set them to have a radius of five pixels each:

```
d3.selectAll("circle")
    .attr("r", 5);
```

Giving us the (not terribly informative) circles shown in Figure 3-1.

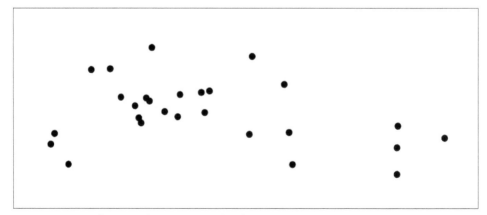

Figure 3-1. Bus collisions with injury versus bus distance between failure

Adding Axes

In order to make this scatter plot a little more informative, we need to introduce axes. The D3 library provides a few axis constructors that do all the heavy lifting. In order to create an axis, we simply pass the constructor the scale object we created above:

```
var x_axis = d3.svg.axis().scale(x_scale);
```

This creates a function which, when called, returns a set of SVG elements that draws the axis, the axis ticks, and tick labels. Because the scale has been passed to the axis, it knows how big it needs to be (the range of the scale) and how to place tick marks along its length. All we need do is maneuver it into place:

```
d3.select("svg")
  .append("g")
    .attr("class", "x axis")
    .attr("transform", "translate(0," + (height-margin) + ")")
  .call(x_axis);
```

Two new things are happening here. The first is that we're using an SVG `transform` to move the axis group down to the bottom of the graph. SVG transforms take an existing element and either rotates them or moves them around. The `translate` transform just moves elements around; it is incredibly useful as we can apply the transform to a group of elements. Here the group of elements that make up the x-axis are moved 0 pixels to the right and `height-margin` pixels down from the top. This means it will coincide with the bottom of our graph; the ticks and tick labels will live in the margin.

 Note that the group element containing the x-axis has been given two classes: x and `axis`. This means we can select the axis using either, or both, of its class names.

The second is that we're using the `.call()` method to actually draw the axis. All this does is call the `time_axis` function, passing in the current selection (the group element) as the argument. Together, these two commands position and draw our x-axis, as shown in Figure 3-2.

We add the y-axis in the same way:

```
var y_axis = d3.svg.axis().scale(y_scale).orient("left");

d3.select("svg")
  .append("g")
    .attr("class", "y axis")
    .attr("transform", "translate(" + margin + ", 0 )")
  .call(y_axis);
```

Unlike the x-axis, here we need to use the `orient` method to set the axis' orientation to "left," and we need to move the y-axis in from the lefthand side of the enclosing element by `margin` pixels. This gives us the graph shown in Figure 3-3.

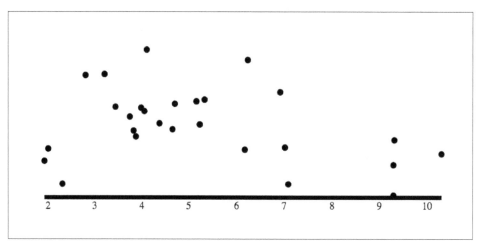

Figure 3-2. Bus collisions with injury versus bus distance between failure—with x-axis

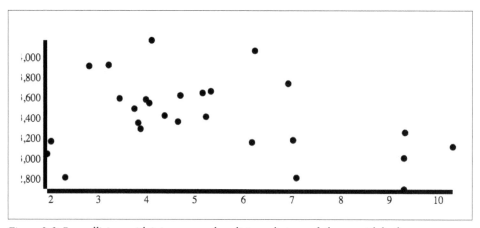

Figure 3-3. Bus collisions with injury versus bus distance between failure—with both axes

We have two glaring aesthetic issues to deal with. The first is that we're chopping off the lefthand side of the y-axis tick labels as they're sticking off the side of the SVG viewport. The second is that Chrome's default rendering of the axes is really ugly! Both these problems are readily solved with some CSS:

```
.axis path{
    fill:none;
    stroke: black;
}
.axis {
    font-size:8pt;
    font-family:sans-serif;
}
.tick {
    fill:none;
```

```
        stroke:black;
    }
    circle{
        stroke:black;
        stroke-width:0.5px;
        fill:RoyalBlue;
        opacity:0.6;
    }
```

This CSS gives us the much more pleasing graph in Figure 3-4. The D3 library focuses on the layout, using scales to let us accurately place data points and axes, leaving the designer to worry about matters of style.

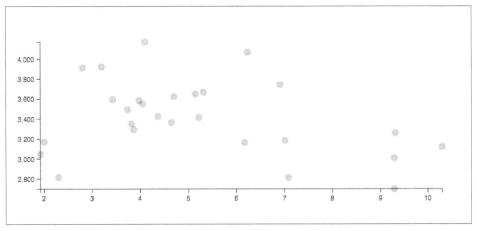

Figure 3-4. Bus collisions with injury versus bus distance between failure—with style

Adding Axis Titles

We need to add axis titles to the axes so that readers can understand the values we're plotting. This isn't taken care of directly by D3, as we can simply place some SVG text elements to do the job. The x-axis is pretty straightforward:

```
d3.select(".x.axis")
  .append("text")
    .text("collisions with injury (per million miles)")
    .attr("x", (width / 2) - margin)
    .attr("y", margin / 1.5);
```

Here we are selecting the x-axis group, appending a text element and specifying its text content as well as its x- and y-coordinates relative to the top-left corner of the group element. The ratios selected were chosen by trying many different ratios and seeing which looked best!

Adding the y-axis title is a little more involved, because we need to rotate and translate the text into place. To rotate SVG text, we specify the amount by which we'd like to rotate, in degrees, and the x- and y-coordinates of the point about which we'd like to rotate. So to place a y-axis title, we create some text at the top of the axis group, specify a rotation that transforms the text through -90 degrees about a point to the left of the top corner of the y-axis group element, and translate the label down into place (see Figure 3-5).

```
d3.select(".y.axis")
    .append("text")
    .text("mean distance between failure (miles)")
    .attr("transform", "rotate (-90, -43, 0) translate(-280)");
```

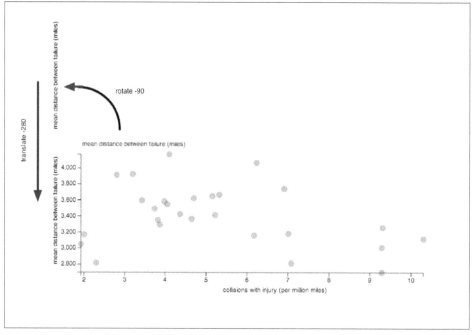

Figure 3-5. Rotating the y-axis label into place—the label is rotated first, then translated into place

This is another example of a situation where Chrome's Developer Tools or Firefox's Firebug are very useful—we can modify the transformations live in the web page and see the results immediately. It's easy to lose elements of the web page off the side of the screen, so being able to play with the transformation values live instead of editing the source code and reloading again and again saves a lot of time.

At this point we have a pretty serviceable scatter chart that implies some relationship between failure and higher injury rates. The relationship, though, is by no means clear —some more analysis is required!

Graphing Turnstile Traffic

Flow into and out of subway stations in New York City is governed by turnstiles. A passenger purchases a ticket and swipes the ticket through the turnstile reader, unlocking the turnstile for one revolution. Each revolution is collected by the MTA and made available publicly.

We will look at the data for the week ending Friday, February 10th, 2012, available at *http://www.mta.info/developers/data/nyct/turnstile/turnstile_120211.txt*. Each line is a day in the life of a set of turnstiles at one part of a station. This file is quite a nightmare to parse: please take a look at the source code of the parser for details. What's important here is that, after severely beating the data into shape, we end up with a JSON file with some approximation to the mean number of people to have passed a turnstile in the Times Square and Grand Central subway stations, two of the largest stations in New York. The resulting JSON is stored in `turnstile_traffic.json`. At its top level it contains two keys, one for `grand_central` and one for `times_square`. Each key points to a list of objects, where an individual object looks like:

```
{
    "count": 87.36111111111111,
    "time": 1328371200000
}
```

Setting up the Viewport

We're going to plot the count of turnstile revolutions against time first as a scatter graph, then introduce lines to connect together the points, giving us a nice time series chart. As above, the first problem we need to overcome is to map the timestamps, which is the number of milliseconds since January 1st 1970, and the mean turnstile revolutions, which range from around 10 to over a thousand, onto a number of pixels on the screen.

We set up our viewport as normal:

```
var margin = 40,
    width = 700 - margin,
    height = 300 - margin;

d3.select("body")
  .append("svg")
    .attr("width", width+margin)
    .attr("width", height+margin)
  .append(g)
    .attr("class","chart");
```

Then let's make two enter selections, one for Times Square and one for Grand Central, and append a bunch of circles to each one:

```
d3.select("svg")
  .selectAll("circle.times_square")
```

```
    .data(data.times_square)
    .enter()
    .append("circle")
      .attr("class", "times_square");

d3.select("svg")
    .selectAll("circle.grand_central")
    .data(data.grand_central)
    .enter()
    .append("circle")
      .attr("class", "grand_central");
```

As in the previous example, we can use a linear scale for the count variable:

```
var count_extent = d3.extent(
    data.times_square.concat(data.grand_central),
    function(d){return d.count}
);

var count_scale = d3.scale.linear()
    .domain(count_extent)
    .range([height, margin]);
```

Note that here we are using `array.concat()`, a general property of JavaScript arrays, which concatenates the two arrays into one. This means that the scale takes into account the data from both data sets. We can use this scale when specifying the y-position of the circles:

```
d3.selectAll("circle")
    .attr("cy", function(d){return count_scale(d.count);});
```

Here the cy property (the y-component of the centre of the circle) is set to the scaled version of the count. We can simply select all circles, independently of their class, as we are applying the same scale to both the .times_square and .grand_central classes.

Creating a Time Scale

A similar approach could be taken with the time axis - we could just build a linear scale that maps the timestamps onto the horizontal extent of the viewport. However, this is going to produce a horribly unreadable time axis (milliseconds since the epoch aren't very human-friendly). Happily, D3 provides a dedicated time axis, which is a linear scale that knows how to deal with time properly. It works in the same way as the linear scale above:

```
var time_extent = d3.extent(
    data.times_square.concat(data.grand_central),
    function(d){return d.time}
);

var time_scale = d3.time.scale()
    .domain(time_extent)
    .range([margin, width]);
```

Again here we are finding the extent of the times (note how the accessor function changed) and then specifying the domain and range of the scale. We use this scale to specify the cx property of the circles:

```
d3.selectAll("circle")
    .attr("cx", function(d){return time_scale(d.time);});
```

Finally, we need to set the radius of the circles. There's no need to continually re-select all the circles as above. If you take a look at the source for this example you'll notice that both scales are created first then the attributes are set in one block:

```
d3.selectAll("circle")
    .attr("cy", function(d){return count_scale(d.count);})
    .attr("cx", function(d){return time_scale(d.time);})
    .attr("r", 3);
```

This is all the browser needs to render our data points! The sad thing is that, as can be seen in Figure 3-6, our visualization has a long way to go before we can learn anything about subway traffic on 42nd Street.

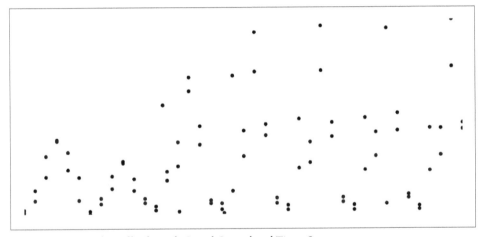

Figure 3-6. Turnstile traffic through Grand Central and Times Square

Adding Axes

This chart needs axes. The most obvious thing about the data so far is that the start of the period is smaller in magnitude than the rest. Are they days? Is the oscillation we can see a diurnal pattern? Are they special days? Explicit x-axis tick marks will let us answer these questions.

We create the axis in the same way as in the previous example, except that now we are creating the axis using a time scale, instead of a linear one:

```
var time_axis = d3.svg.axis()
    .scale(time_scale);
```

Because the scale object is a *time* scale object D3 intelligently chooses appropriately located tick marks and nice tick labels, appropriate to the extent of the time in the data set.

We place it, as before, by creating an SVG group element, moving that group element into the correct location and then calling the `time_axis` function:

```
d3.select("svg")
  .append("g")
  .attr("class", "x axis")
  .attr("transform", "translate(0," + height + ")")
  .call(time_axis);
```

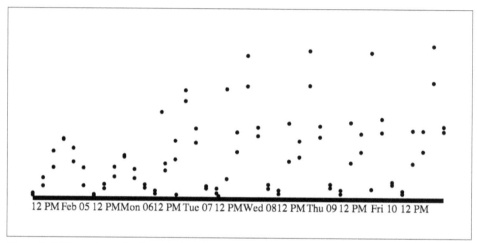

Figure 3-7. Turnstile traffic through Grand Central and Times Square, with an x-axis.

We're starting to be able to see that the lower amount of traffic is occurring over the weekend, and that the oscillations we can see are indeed diurnal. Let's add the y-axis (note the extra **orient** command):

```
var count_axis = d3.svg.axis()
  .scale(count_scale)
  .orient("left");

d3.select("svg")
  .append("g")
  .attr("class", "y axis")
  .attr("transform", "translate(" + margin + ",0)")
  .call(count_axis);
```

and some desperately needed style:

```
.axis {
    font-family: arial;
    font-size:0.6em;
}
path {
```

```
    fill:none;
    stroke:black;
    stroke-width:2px;
}
.tick {
    fill:none;
    stroke:black;
}
circle{
    stroke:black;
    stroke-width:0.5px;
}
circle.times_square{
    fill:DeepPink;
}
circle.grand_central{
    fill:MediumSeaGreen;
}
```

to get Figure 3-8. This is starting to look acceptable, though our graph is still a few lines and axis labels away from presentable. Let's turn this into a more traditional time-series graph by introducing a line to join the dots.

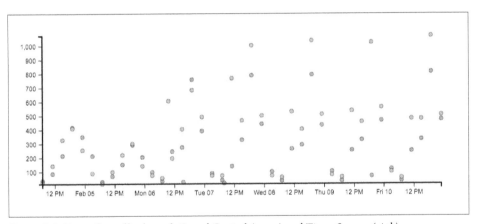

Figure 3-8. Turnstile traffic through Grand Central (green) and Times Square (pink).

Adding A Path

A path is a continuous line with one or more segments. They're a bit of a pain to set up manually using SVG, though this is not something that need concern us as D3 provides a path generator that does the heavy lifting. We use the path constructor in the same way we use the axis constructor:

```
var line = d3.svg.line()
    .x(function(d){return time_scale(d.time)})
    .y(function(d){return count_scale(d.count)});
```

Here d3.svg.line() generates a function that takes in a data set and outputs an SVG path element. We specify the .x() and .y() accessor methods using the scales we created so that we can pass the data set into line and get back a path that has been appropriately scaled into pixels.

The line object can now be called as though it were a function and we call it by passing in all the appropriate data at once.

```
d3.select("svg")
  .append("path")
    .attr("d", line(data.times_square))
    .attr("class", "times_square");

d3.select("svg")
  .append("path")
    .attr("d", line(data.grand_central))
    .attr("class", "grand_central");
```

The whole path is a single SVG element, so we don't follow the normal selectAll, data, enter idiom, which would normally allow us to generate a large set of elements. Here we pass all the data into the line function, which generates the path.

To finish off this visualization we need axis labels:

```
d3.select(".y.axis")
    .append("text")
    .text("mean number of turnstile revolutions")
    .attr("transform", "rotate (90, " + -margin + ", 0)")
    .attr("x", 20)
    .attr("y", 0);

d3.select(".x.axis")
    .append("text")
    .text("time")
    .attr("x", function(){return (width / 1.6) - margin})
    .attr("y", margin/1.5);
```

and a bit more CSS to make the lines appropriately color coded:

```
path.times_square{
    stroke:DeepPink;
}
path.grand_central{
    stroke:MediumSeaGreen;
}
```

which gives us the plot in Figure 3-9. This plot is now starting to show some really interesting dynamics in the turnstile traffic. We can see, for example, that Times Square consistently lags behind Grand Central, that weekday traffic at Grand Central has a much more prominent morning rush-hour peak, and that Thursday's data at Times Square is curiously low, suggesting something may have skewed that day's results.

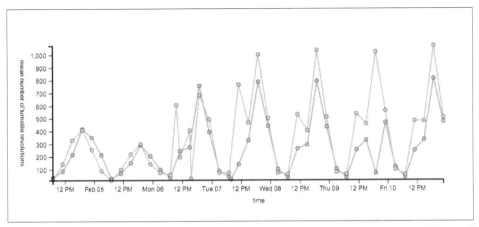

Figure 3-9. Turnstile traffic through Grand Central (green) and Times Square (pink)—with lines and axis labels.

CHAPTER 4

Interaction and Transitions

So far, we have reproduced the basics: lists, bar charts, scatter graphs, and line charts. While it's important to have these fundamental building blocks in our toolkit, arguably we've not done a great deal more than one could do with standard graphing libraries. The key difference between D3 and earlier generation graphing methods is that our canvas is a web page in a modern browser—a piece of technology that is fundamentally interactive. This means that, with very little effort, we can introduce basic user interactions using standard browser events. By combining interaction with D3's capability to animate the elements of the web page, we are able to build up rich visualizations that would have been next to impossible with earlier tools.

A Subway Wait Assessment UI I—Interactions

The MTA Subway Wait Assessment is defined as "the percent of actual intervals between trains that are no more than the scheduled interval plus 25%" (i.e., the percentage of trains that were more or less on time). The data is collected once a month and made available, per subway line, to the public. We are going to create a User Interface (UI) using D3 in order to help the public explore this data.

The aim for this example is to provide a simple UI that allows a user to investigate and compare the data, to explore the data in more detail via interaction. This is a very powerful way of presenting data, as it allows the user to choose what they feel is important, and what will help them make decisions. Ben Shneiderman has been teaching this for at least 15 years: "Overview first, zoom and filter, then details-on-demand."[1] With D3 we can achieve this sort of interaction without much more work than we've already done in earlier chapters.

---

1. Ben Shneiderman. A Thousand Fold Increase in Human Capabilities. Educom Review, 32, 6 (Nov/Dec 1997), 4-10.

There are two data sets we're going to use in this example. One is the top-level summary statistics data, called *subway_wait_mean.json*, of which one entry looks like the following:

```
{
    "line_id": "6_Line"
    "line_name": "6 Line",
    "mean": 73.400000000000006
}
```

The second data set is the lower-level detail, which contains the subway wait assessment at a monthly level for the last year. The file is called 'subway_wait.json' and an individual record from that looks like:

```
{
    "line_id": 1_Line
    "line_name": "1 Line",
    "late_percent": 73.1,
    "month": 1
}
```

A Robust Viewport Setup

We're going to build a time series graph where the user can select those time series they'd like to see. The wait assessment available online right now runs from 2009 through to spring of 2011. We have 22 separate lines excluding the shuttles (which seem to be on-schedule most of the time!), motivating the interactive piece of this graph: showing all the lines at once would be a bit of a mess! We will have a time series plot on the left hand side of the screen, with a clickable key of lines on the righthand side. This example will have a slightly more complex layout than the earlier examples, so we sketch out the structure first shown in Example 4-1.

Example 4-1. Structure of the time series UI layout

```
<div id="timeseries">
    <svg>
        <g id="chart">
        </g>
    </svg>
</div>

<div id="key">
    <div class="key_line">
        <div class="key_square">
        </div>
        <div class="key_label">
        </div>
    </div>
    <div class="key_line">
        <div class="key_square">
        </div>
        <div class="key_label">
```

```
        </div>
    </div>
    ...
</div>
```

So we will have two top-level `div` tags, with IDs `timeseries` and `key`. Inside the key will be one row per subway line, containing the `key_line` div tag, which in turn contains the `key_square`, which will have color code and the `key_label`, which will have the line name.

The time series plots will all live inside the `timeseries` div tag, which is, in turn, inside the `svg` element. This example uses a more robust idiom for placing the plot elements —the plot will live inside an SVG group element, which will be positioned inside the root SVG element to take into account the necessary margins for the axis ticks and labels.

We begin with the following HTML, which has two extra `div` tags and some basic style:

```
<!DOCTYPE html>
<html>
<head>
    <meta charset="utf-8"i/>
    <script type="text/javascript" src="d3.js"></script>
</head>
<style>
    .axis path, line{
        stroke:black;
    }
    .line {
        float:left;
    }
    .line_container{
        width: 150px;
        height: 20px;
    }
    path{
        fill: none;
    }
    .key{
        float:right;
    }
    .key_line{
        font-size:17px;
        width:100%;
    }
    .key_square{
        height:10px;
        width:10px;
        outline:solid 1px black;
        float:left;
        margin: 6px 10px 0px 10px;
    }
    #timeseries{
        float:left;
```

```
            }
        >
        <script>
        function draw(data){
                // script starts here
        }
        </script>
        <body>
            <div id="timeseries"></div>
            <div id="key"></div>
            <script>
                d3.json("data/subway_wait_mean.json", draw);
            </script>
        </body>
        </html>
```

which sets up the top-level divs. The CSS in this example lives in the top **style** tag and the JavaScript lives in the top **script** tag. The first thing we will do in the script is set up the SVG viewport. So, inside the **draw** function:

```
var container_dimensions = {width: 900, height: 400},
    margins = {top: 10, right: 20, bottom: 30, left: 60},
    chart_dimensions = {
        width: container_dimensions.width - margins.left - margins.right,
        height: container_dimensions.height - margins.top - margins.bottom
    };

var chart = d3.select("#timeseries")
  .append("svg")
    .attr("width", container_dimensions.width)
    .attr("height", container_dimensions.height)
  .append("g")
    .attr("transform", "translate(" + margins.left + "," + margins.top + ")")
    .attr("id","chart");
```

A number of new things are happening here. First, we specify two sets of dimensions: the dimensions of the SVG container and then the dimensions of the chart itself. The point here is that we build the chart inside an SVG group with enough space around the edges of the group for the axis and axis labels to live in, avoiding annoying corrections later on in the script. Having set up the dimensions, we add an SVG element to the page, then a group element, which is translated right and down by the appropriate number of pixels.

We have also assigned a selection to a variable for the first time. Each **append** returns the D3 selection of that element, so here we are assigning the selection of the g element to the **chart** variable. This avoids having to continually reselect the chart group to hang new elements from it.

Next, we need to set up scales and axes, which we do as usual. The one difference here is that we are manually setting the domains of the scales rather than using the extent of the data set. In this case we know the domains ahead of time, and want to frame all the different time series nicely:

```
var time_scale = d3.time.scale()
    .range([0,chart_dimensions.width])
    .domain([new Date(2008, 0, 1), new Date(2011, 3, 1)]);

var percent_scale = d3.scale.linear()
    .range([chart_dimensions.height, 0])
    .domain([65,90]);

var time_axis = d3.svg.axis()
    .scale(time_scale);

var count_axis = d3.svg.axis()
    .scale(percent_scale)
    .orient("left");

chart.append("g")
    .attr("class", "x axis")
    .attr("transform", "translate(0," + chart_dimensions.height + ")")
    .call(time_axis);

chart.append("g")
    .attr("class", "y axis")
    .call(count_axis);

d3.select(".y.axis")
  .append("text")
    .attr("text-anchor","middle")
    .text("percent on time")
    .attr("transform", "rotate (-270, 0, 0)")
    .attr("x", container.height/2)
    .attr("y", 50);
```

Next we need to build the key. For this we will use the summary JSON and iterate through in much the same way as we did for the bar chart in Chapter 2. Note that the draw function is called with this summary JSON file as its **data** variable. We first append the div.key_line tags and store the resulting selection in a variable:

```
var key_items = d3.select("#key")
  .selectAll("div")
  .data(data)
  .enter()
  .append("div")
    .attr("class","key_line")
    .attr("id",function(d){return d.line_id});
```

Note that each div has the same class but a unique ID. The key_items variable now stores the selection of all the elements of class .key_line with their associated data. Using this variable it becomes easy to hang the .key_square and .key_label elements from each key_line element:

```
key_items.append("div")
    .attr("id", function(d){return "key_square_" + d.line_id})
    .attr("class", "key_square");

key_items.append("div")
```

```
        .attr("class","key_label")
        .text(function(d){return d.line_name});
```

This gives us our empty (and not terribly well-styled) stage shown in Figure 4-1. We now need to add some interaction to allow the user to choose which line to draw.

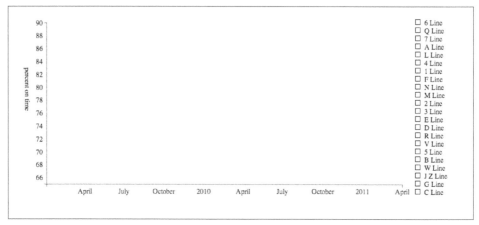

Figure 4-1. Empty axes and key

Adding Interaction

The browser is constantly firing events in response to user behavior. Every time the user passes their mouse over an element, a mouseover event is fired in the context of that element. Every time a user clicks on an element, a mousedown event is fired as the mouse button is depressed, a mouseup event is fired as the mouse button is released, and a click event is fired immediately thereafter.

The browser is capable of firing a large number of events (see the DOM Level 2 Events Specification for a full list) though the examples below will focus on the "click" and "mouseover" events. For each element in the page, we can register an event handler that listens for a specific type of event emanating from that element and then, when the event is fired, runs a callback function that performs the desired actions. The D3 library provides a handy .on() method that can be called on a selection, attaching an event handler to the elements in that selection.

We'll start by adding a click event to the .key_line elements:

```
d3.selectAll(".key_line")
    .on("click", get_timeseries_data);
```

This simply says for each .key_line element in the selection, add an event handler that listens for the click event and, when that event is fired, call get_timeseries_data, which we will write next. The function is referred to as the "listener" and is called just like all the other callbacks, with that element's data passed in as the first argument, the index

---

as the second (always referred to herein and elsewhere as d and i). Importantly, it also sets the this keyword to be the element to which we've attached the handler.

 The this keyword is a notorious stumbling block when learning Java-Script. Generally, its value is dependent on the execution context and the syntax of the function call. When using callbacks in D3, this is always set to the current element, allowing us to select the element directly while inside the callback. It's always worth using con sole.log(this) in more complex situations, if only to make sure you're not going crazy!

The callback's job is to toggle the timeseries line on and off as the key gets clicked on. In order to do this, it will need to test if the line exists already on the page and, if not, fetch the timeseries data and draw the requested time series. Here's the callback that performs this check and filters the JSON file for the requested time-series data:

```
function get_timeseries_data(){
    // get the id of the current element
    var id = d3.select(this).attr("id");  ❶
    // see if we have an associated time series
    var ts = d3.select("#"+id+"_path");
    if (ts.empty()){  ❷
        d3.json("data/subway_wait.json", function(data){
            filtered_data = data.filter(function(d){return d.line_id === id});  ❸
            draw_timeseries(filtered_data, id);
        })
    } else {
        ts.remove();  ❹
    }
}
```

There are four new things going on here:

❶ We have selected the element that was clicked on using the this keyword. This gives us access to its ID, which is how we tie everything together.

❷ We have used D3's selection.empty() to test if the selection we made actually contains any elements. If the line had not been drawn, then the selection ts is empty and ts.empty() will return true. In this case, we then need to extract the data for that line and draw it. If, on the other hand, the line had already been drawn, the selection stored in ts will contain the line elements, and ts.empty() will return false. In this case, we need to simply remove the line in the selection from the visualization.

❸ We have used JavaScript's array.filter() method to pick out the data whose ID is equal to the ID of the current element. The .filter() method works simply by evaluating the callback function on each element of the data set, keeping only those elements that return true. This is a bit of a shortcut; ideally we'd only request the data we needed, keeping the memory footprint of the page lower.

❹ We have used D3's `selection.remove()` method to remove the element if it already exists on the page. This simply removes all the elements in the selection from the page.

Having filtered out the correct data we call **draw_timeseries** passing in the data and the ID. This function is very simple, it just draws the line defined by the data. The problem, though, is that as it stands we do not have access to the scale objects we created when setting the stage above. We need to make the scale objects global, which requires two edits. The first, is that we need to declare the scale objects outside the **draw** function, inside the **script** tags:

```
<script>
var time_scale,
    percent_scale;

function draw(data){
    ...
```

This declares two global variables that can be accessed anywhere inside the JavaScript on this page. The second is we need to go to where we defined the scales and remove the **var** keyword when we assign the variable names to the scale objects:

```
time_scale = d3.time.scale()
    .range([0,chart_dimensions.width])
    .domain([new Date(2008, 0, 1), new Date(2011, 3, 1)]);

percent_scale = d3.scale.linear()
    .range([chart_dimensions.height, 0])
    .domain([65,90]);
```

This prevents them from being defined only in the scope of the **draw** function, making them available to our **draw_timeseries** function, which is now simply:

```
function draw_timeseries(data, id){

    var line = d3.svg.line()
        .x(function(d){return time_scale(d.time)})
        .y(function(d){return percent_scale(d.late_percent)})
        .interpolate("linear");

    var g = d3.select("#chart")
        .append("g")
        .attr("id", id + "_path")
        .attr("class", id.split("_")[1]);

    g.append("path")
        .attr("d", line(data));
}
```

Note that there's a seemingly unnecessary SVG group element in there. This has been dropped in for the example in the next section, where we shall add in some transitions. For now, though, we have a fully functional interactive visualization! When the user clicks on a **key_line**, they will now get to see the wait assessment over 2009 and 2010 corresponding to that subway line. Figure 4-2 shows the result of clicking on the 4, 5, and 6 lines—something happened in January of 2011 that caused a sharp drop in the punctuality of these lines!

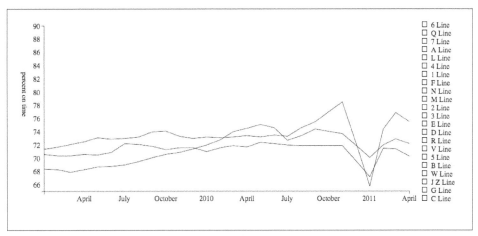

Figure 4-2. Wait assessment for the 4, 5, and 6 subway lines

Subway Wait Assessment UI II—Transitions

We have now made a user interface that is serviceable—it provides a basic way for a user to explore the MTA Subway Wait Assessment data. However, we can introduce a richer level of interaction by using a few basic animations, known as "transitions" in D3. Transitions work by changing properties of the web page element, typically by transitioning between one set of properties to another in a smooth manner.

We can use transitions to highlight important aspects of our data, especially when time is involved, to advertise the fact that something should be clicked on, to keep track of constant elements in the visualization[2], or to just be downright flashy. In practice we should stick exclusively to the first three uses, though in this section we will let ourselves get ever so slightly carried away and make something a little cheesy.

A Simple Interactive Transition

A useful interaction for someone who needs to find out individual values is to provide a small label when the user mouseovers the data point. So let's start by throwing in some circles for each data point. Inside the `draw_timeseries` function, after we've added in the path, we can easily throw in some circles:

```
g.selectAll("circle")
  .data(data)
```

2. See *http://bost.ocks.org/mike/constancy/* for more on constancy.

```
    .enter()
    .append("circle")
      .attr("cx", function(d) {return time_scale(d.time)})
      .attr("cy", function(d) {return percent_scale(d.late_percent)})
      .attr("r",5);
```

The first transition we will build is a simple mouseover transition, that will grow the circle a bit to give the user some visual feedback as to the fact that the graph is inter- active. The code is nice and straightforward, transitions being one of D3's strengths:

```
g.selectAll("circle")
    .on("mouseover", function(d){
        d3.select(this)
            .transition()
            .attr("r",9);
    })
    .on("mouseout", function(d){
        d3.select(this)
            .transition()
            .attr("r",5);
    });
```

The transition method smoothly interpolates between the initial condition of an at- tribute to the value specified after the transition. So in our case, during the mouseover we transition from a radius of 5px to a radius of 9px. On mouseout we transition back down to 5px.

Adding Mouseover Labels

Let's add a tool tip-style label for the data point so the user can get a more accurate reading by inspection. We shall simply have the tool tip appear on mouseover:

```
g.selectAll("circle")
    .on("mouseover.tooltip", function(d){
        d3.select("text#" + d.line_id).remove();
        d3.select("#chart")
            .append("text")
            .text(d.late_percent + "%")
            .attr("x", time_scale(d.time) + 10)
            .attr("y", percent_scale(d.late_percent) - 10)
            .attr("id", d.line_id);
    });
```

Nothing terribly new here: we append an SVG text element just up and to the right of the circle and set the id of the text to the line_id. The one odd-looking line here is first line in the mouseover callback; before we add a new tool tip, we remove any tool tips that already exist on that line. This is good practice if we know we only ever want one tool tip on at a time, and also corrects any corner-case interaction bugs that can occur if the transition below is interrupted.

On mouseout we shall fade the label out and, because it is so easy to get carried away with transitions, we shall transform the position of the label up and to the right a bit, giving the label fade a bit of drama:

```
g.selectAll("circle")
    .on("mouseout.tooltip", function(d){
        d3.select("text." + d.line_id)
            .transition()
            .duration(500)
            .style("opacity",0)
            .attr("transform","translate(10, -10)")
            .remove();
    });
```

Here we transition to 0 opacity, transition from `translate(0,0)` to `translate(10,-10)` and then, at the end of the transition, remove the element from the page. Note that here the duration of the transition is set explicitly to 500ms. This gives the transition ever so slightly more time to perform the interpolation than the default of 250ms. These two transitions occur at the same time as each other, and over the same 500ms period. We end up with a time series with responsive, informative data points, shown in Figure 4-3.

 The `.remove()` method works a little differently on a transition. When called on a selection, remove immediately removes the element. When called on a transition, the `.remove()` method runs only at the end of the transition.

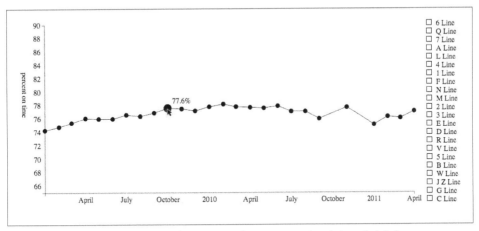

Figure 4-3. A simple mouseover, with responsive data points and tool tip-style labels

An Entry Animation Using Delays

It's often useful to highlight the fact that something is interactive, which is often simply drawing the users attention to it. To do this, we're going to introduce the circles, one after the other, in a quick animation when the user chooses a line. It would be easy to go overboard with this animation, though here that's left as an exercise for the reader.

Before we do anything, we need to alter the appending code above in "A Simple Inter-active Transition" on page 41. Instead of adding circles with a radius of 5, we add them in with a radius of 0px, so they can't be seen. We then immediately run:

```
var enter_duration = 1000;
g.selectAll("circle")
    .transition()
    .delay(function(d, i) { return i / data.length * enter_duration; })
    .attr("r", 5);
```

Here the `.delay()` method is used to delay the transition by the number of specified milliseconds. This code generates a per-element delay that increases as the index into the set of circles increases. The index starts at zero, meaning that the first circle appears immediately. The second circle starts with index one so, because we have 26 elements, the delay is 1/26th of a second, the third circle starts after 2/26ths of a second and so on. As our data comes ordered by time, setting the delay to be per-item in this manner gives the impression that the circles appear quickly one by one over the course of a second. A screen capture of this animation is shown in Figure 4-4.

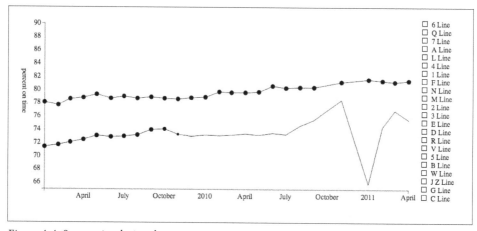

Figure 4-4. Some point during the entry transition

Adding Line Labels

The last thing we shall add to this UI before styling it is to put a label at the end of the line. We'd like to do this after the circles have appeared along the length of the line. We shall use the final circle to give the line a label by making it a little bigger than the others and adding some text indicating which line it is. After we style this it will look like the MTA subway symbol!

In order to draw this *after* the entry animation, we need to use the .each() method at the end of the entry transition. So, here's the entry animation again except this time we call some more code that will take place after the transition has completed:

```
g.selectAll("circle")
    .transition()
    .delay(function(d, i) { return i / data.length * enter_duration; })
    .attr("r", 5)
    .each("end",function(d,i){
        if (i === data.length-1){
            add_label(this,d);
        }
    });
```

The .each() method is called for each element in the transition, and takes as its first argument either "start" or "end". If "start" is specified the callback in the second argument will be fired at the start of the transition. If "end" is specified the callback will be triggered once the transition has completed. This is commonly used to chain together animation events.

The callback first checks to see if the current element is the final circle in the array. If it is, the function below is called, which makes that circle a bit bigger and fades in the label:

```
function add_label(circle, d){
    d3.select(circle)
        .transition()
        .attr("r", 9);
    g.append("text")
        .text(d.line_id.split("_")[1])
        .attr("x", time_scale(d.time))
        .attr("y", percent_scale(d.late_percent))
        .attr("dy", "0.35em")
        .attr("class","linelabel")
        .attr("text-anchor","middle")
        .style("opacity", 0)
        .style("fill", "white")
        .transition()
            .style("opacity", 1);
}
```

The .attr("dy", "0.35em") serves to vertically center the SVG text in the line label. It's a bit magical, but is better supported than the dominant-baseline style.

This gives us some nice line labels, shown in Figure 4-5. They appear after the circles have populated the line, and they fade in nicely. Finally, we need to tell the browser to not shrink the circles on mouseout, using:

```
g.selectAll("circle")
    .on("mouseout", function(d,i){
        if (i !== data.length-1) {
            d3.select(this).transition().attr("r", 5);
        }
    })
```

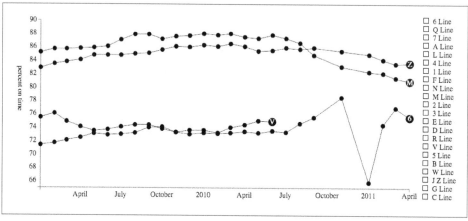

Figure 4-5. Time series showing subway line labels

Style

We can't, in good conscience, leave the graph as it is. Stylewise it's still a disaster, and we can make it so much nicer without much effort. First, we have train_colours.css, which contains all the official MTA subway colors, using rules like:

```
.Line_1, .Line_2, .Line_3{
    stroke:#EE352E;
    fill:#EE352E;
    background-color:#EE352E;
}
```

Hopefully you noticed that we set each line's group class, and each key_square's class, to be compatible with stylesheet so simply by including it we get a marked improvement in the look of the UI. A final touch of CSS finishes off this example:

```
.timeseries path{
    stroke-width:3px;
}
.timeseries circle{
    stroke: white;
}
.timeseries text{
    fill: white;
```

```
    stroke: none;
    font-size:12px;
    font-weight: bold;
}
```

This produces the screenshot in Figure 4-6, allowing us to investigate the wait assessment of each subway over time.

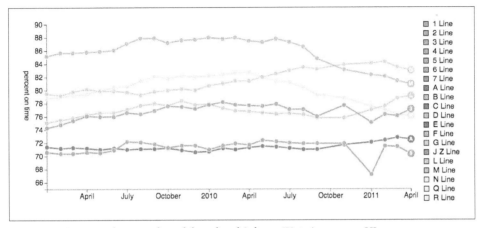

Figure 4-6. An example screenshot of the colored Subway Wait Assessment UI

CHAPTER 5

Layout

All the examples so far have focused on D3's ability to join a data set with elements of a web page. We have seen the `.selectAll('element').data(data).enter().append('element')` idiom over and over again in each example, and it is getting used to this idiom that really constitutes D3's learning curve. Having been thoroughly exposed to this idiom, this getting started guide will finish with a light exploration of two of D3's many layout tools. The aim of this last set of examples is to hint at the great range of possibilities opened up by D3, and how easy it is to use these tools. For many more beautiful examples visit *http://d3js.org*.

Subway Connectivity

The MTA provides a set of General Transit Feed Specification (GTFS) files for each form of transit in New York that it controls. These are used by (among others) Google to provide services such as map overlays, distance calculations, and schedule displays. These files are wonderfully constructed and well documented at *https://developers.google.com/transit/gtfs/*—a real pleasure to play with!

With minimal fuss, we are able to join the `stops.txt` and `stop_times.txt` files in order to create a record of which stations are connected to one another. This data is stored in `stations_graph.json` and contains two lists. One is called `nodes`, an individual element of which looks like the following:

```
{
    "name": "St George"
}
```

The other is called `links`, an individual element of which looks like the following:

```
{
    "source": 0,
    "target": 264
},
```

Here the nodes represent stations, for which we store the name, and links represent the fact that one can travel between the two stations. For each link we store the node index of the starting station and the end station. The overall structure of the file is then:

```
{
    "links": [
        {
            "source": 0,
            "target": 264
        },
        {
            "source": 0,
            "target": 6
        },
        ...
    ],
    "nodes": [
        {
            "name": "St George"
        },
        {
            "name": "Hunts Point Av"
        },
        ...
    ]
}
```

Force Directed Graphs

We're going to draw the graph represented by the JSON data set above. Subway stations are nodes which shall be represented as SVG circles; connections between subways are edges, which shall be represented as SVG lines. D3's `layout.force()` tools make laying out, animating, and making such a graph interactive very straightforward.

First, we lay out the circles and edges:

```
var width = 1500,
    height = 1500;

var svg = d3.select("body")
  .append("svg")
    .attr("width", width)
    .attr("height", height);

var node = svg.selectAll("circle.node")
  .data(data.nodes)
  .enter()
  .append("circle")
    .attr("class", "node")
    .attr("r", 12);

var link = svg.selectAll("line.link")
  .data(data.links)
```

```
    .enter().append("line")
    .style("stroke","black");
```

This populates the web page with the appropriate elements, we just need to lay them out. The `force` layout applies a force-directed algorithm to decide the position of each node. Here, each node feels a repulsive force from every other node, but is constrained by the edges that keep nodes connected together. This can result in an organic layout that looks wonderfully inviting as it unfolds. D3 makes it easy; first we instantiate the algorithm:

```
var force = d3.layout.force()
    .charge(-120)
    .linkDistance(30)
    .size([width, height])
    .nodes(data.nodes)
    .links(data.links)
    .start();
```

These methods are all custom methods for the algorithm that detail the various parameters and references the algorithm needs to compute how the position of the nodes and edges should change. We then use it to modify the appropriate attributes of our lines and circles:

```
force.on("tick", function() {
    link.attr("x1", function(d) { return d.source.x; })
        .attr("y1", function(d) { return d.source.y; })
        .attr("x2", function(d) { return d.target.x; })
        .attr("y2", function(d) { return d.target.y; });

    node.attr("cx", function(d) { return d.x; })
        .attr("cy", function(d) { return d.y; });
});
```

The layout algorithm generates a tick event, which corresponds to a single step of the layout algorithm. It also provides the `.on()` method, which listens for these tick events and is used to update the positions of the nodes and edges. The algorithm provides the position of the nodes and edges as data to the `.on()` method's callback.

 With D3's more advanced layout tools, it can be a little difficult to tell what data is available to you in a callback. A quick way to solve this is using `console.log()`. In the callback you're building, try writing `function(d,i){console.log(d); // code you're trying to write}`, which will then print the data assigned to each element you're trying to modify in the JavaScript console.

Finally, a common feature of graph visualization is the ability to drag the nodes around as the algorithm runs, allowing the user to investigate the network's properties in a very interactive manner. Here's the code:

```
node.call(force.drag);
```

This simply binds a set of mouse events to the nodes that allows the user to interact with the graph. D3 creates these events carefully so that any other mouse events that we create and assign to the nodes of the graph still work fine. All this gives us a nice interactive graph shown in Figure 5-1 that shows how the subways in New York are connected. The network is fully connected apart from the Staten Island subway, which can be seen on its own at the bottom of the screen.

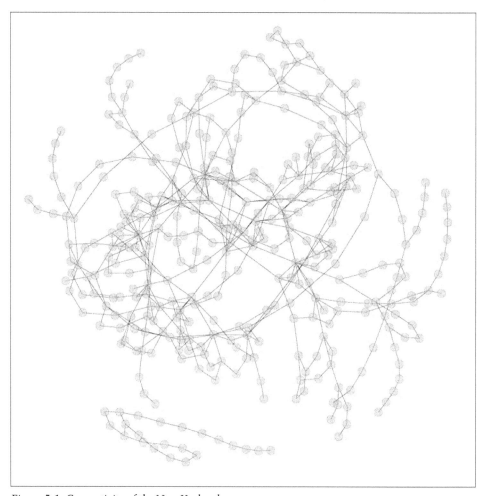

Figure 5-1. Connectivity of the New York subway

Scheduled Wait Time Distribution

The GTFS data contains all the scheduled stops at each subway station, stored in `stop_times.txt`. By joining this with `trips.txt` we are able to find the time between the scheduled arrival times of a set of five subway lines. The JSON that we form is therefore an array with five elements, one per train line. Each element contains the interarrival times in minutes across all the stops, across the whole schedule:

```
[
    {
        "interarrival_times": [
            19.0,
            20.0,
            ...
            20.0,
            20.0
        ],
        "route_id": "F"
    },
    ...
]
```

We are going to use the `d3.layout.histogram()` layout to bin the counts of each wait time for a set of train lines, and the `d3.layout.stack()` to draw them on top of each other.

Using the Histogram Layout

Our data set contains many tens of thousands of data points, each of which represents a scheduled interarrival time. We can use a histogram to estimate and plot the distribution of these times. D3's `histogram` layout does the heavy lifting of counting each data point and placing it into the appropriate bin. First we set up the layout:

```
var histogram = d3.layout.histogram()
    .bins(d3.range(1.5, 23 , 2.2))
    .frequency(false);
```

This creates an object that we can use to organize our observations, which we are treating as continuous into bins. The `.bins()` method specifies the lower bound of each bin, using the `d3.range()` utility function, which here generates a set of bins from 1.5 to 23 in steps of 2.2. The `.frequency()` method tells D3 to calculate a normalized histogram, as opposed to just calculating the count in each bin. This is important as we're interested in how the wait times are distributed rather than the raw count of wait times, which is more to do with the number of stops on a line.

In general, it's not great to pick histogram bins arbitrarily. Here the bin edges have been chosen by trial and error, reducing this statistical validity of the visualization (sometimes known as an "art project"). If the `.bins()` method is omitted then Sturges' formula[1] is used which makes some statistical assumptions about the data, and will bin the data on a per-line basis. However, as we need to compare bins across subway lines, we are forcing the bins to be the same across lines.

---

1. Sturges, H. A. (1926). "The choice of a class interval." J American Statistical Association: 65–66. JSTOR 2965501.

We apply the histogram layout to the data as though it were a function:

```
var counts = data.map(
    function(d){
        return histogram(d.interarrival_times)
    }
);
```

which results in a new data set that contains the lower bound x, width dx, and height y of each bar in the histogram. If we had only one subway line to visualize, we could simply use these data points to draw the histogram using SVG rect elements. However, we have five subway lines to visualize, so we are going to stack them on top of each other.

Using the Stack Layout

By stacking the bars for each individual line on top of each other we are able to see two things all at once: the overall distribution of wait times for the five subway lines, and the relative wait time for each line. In order to actually draw it, we use the d3.lay out.stack() layout, which gives us, for each bar, a baseline d.y0 that we can use to draw the stack. We initialize the stack layout, as in both the histogram and the force-directed graph, by creating the layout object:

```
var stack = d3.layout.stack();
```

We don't need to specify any accessors or settings, as we're building on top of the histogram objects that use the default names for the x- and y-properties of the bars. If we were using names other than the default, we'd need to create .x() and .y() accessors for this layout. We are also using the default offset, which specifies how the baseline of the stack behaves. We need it to be aligned to the y-axis, but other streamgraph settings often use a centered layout for some impressive layouts.

All we really need to do is pass the counts variable we made above to the stack layout. This will bless our data with a y0 property, which we can use in the layout:

```
svg.selectAll("g")
  .data(stack(counts))
  .enter()
  .append("g")
    .attr("class",function(d,i){return lines[i]})
  .selectAll("rect")
  .data(function(d){return d})
  .enter()
  .append("rect")
    .attr("x",function(d){return x_scale(d.x) })
    .attr("y",function(d){return count_scale(d.y) - (height - margin -
count_scale(d.y0))})
    .attr("width", function(d){return x_scale(d.x + d.dx) - x_scale(d.x)})
    .attr("height", function(d){return height - margin - count_scale(d.y)});
```

There's nothing new in the above code, though it is a little finicky. The stack(counts) data set is an array with five elements, for each we make and SVG group.

For each group we need to join the contents of that element, which contains all the data we need to draw the individual layer of the stack, to a bunch of rectangles. So we use the `.data()` method again to access this second level of the data.

Note how we use `d.y0` to adjust the y position of the rectangle upwards, effectively stacking the bars on top of each other. Adding in an x-axis and a bit of style gives us the bar chart in Figure 5-2, which starts to explain a bit more about how New Yorkers feel about the various lines. We can see that the L-train is likely to give you the shortest wait time, and that the G-train (affectionately known as the "Ghost" Train) is scheduled for longer waits.

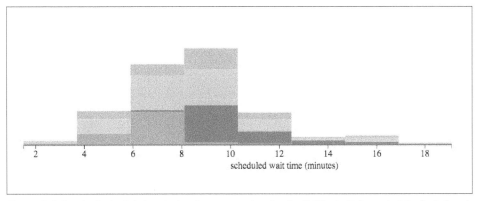

Figure 5-2. Stacked scheduled wait time between trains for the C (blue), G (green), 1 (red), L (grey), and F (orange) trains

CHAPTER 6

Conclusion

The aim of this book was to introduce the basic aspects of using D3. We have seen how to build up and serve simple visualizations using both HTML and SVG. We've seen how D3 allows us to join together elements of data set with elements of a web page, and how we can modify the attributes of those web page elements based on the data. We've used D3's scale objects to map data values onto pixels and colors. We've used D3's axis and line generators to simplify the basic aspects of building visualizations, and D3's interaction and transitions capabilities to create an engaging UI. Finally, we touched on some more complex tools that D3 provides in order to lay out more demanding, modern visualizations.

What Next?

This book has scraped only the surface of D3, there is a lot more to be explored. A good place to start reading further is Mike Bostock's blog posts on all sorts of aspects of D3 available at *http://bost.ocks.org/mike/*. These posts go into depth on some more advanced topics, and provide a great selection of examples, talks, and academic articles. Of particular note are those articles that talk about best practices, which become very important as you make more serious visualizations for publication.

The documentation for D3 is extensive, and is available at *http://d3js.org* along with a huge gallery of examples. This is an essential resource, both for reference and inspiration.

Finally, the community around D3 is very active and friendly, and growing fast. The `d3-js` user group is a great resource for conversation and the `d3.js` tag on Stack Overflow should be used for specific questions.

About the Author

Mike Dewar is a data scientist at Bitly, a New York tech company that makes long URLs shorter. He has a PhD in modelling dynamic systems from data from the University of Sheffield in the UK, and has worked as a Machine Learning post-doc in The University of Edinburgh and Columbia University. He has been drawing graphs regularly since he was in high school, and is starting to get the hang of it.

Lightning Source UK Ltd.
Milton Keynes UK
UKHW031818050422
401139UK00005B/308

9 781449 328795